I0108362

ABIGAIL ROSE VISITS
The Gamble Plantation

AN EARLY READER ADVENTURE

WRITTEN BY LELA RAST HARTSAW

PHOTO-ILLUSTRATED BY MICHELLE DONNER

COPYRIGHT ©2016
By
Lela Rast Hartsaw

All rights reserved.

ISBN# 0692808809
ISBN-13# 978-0692808801

For information on speaking engagements
or curriculum adaptation, please contact the author:
whatsmamawriting@gmail.com
Visit her website: whatsmamawriting.com

DEDICATION:
This book is dedicated to the Gamble and Patten Families
and the many people who helped settle Manatee County.

Design/Layout: Lela Rast Hartsaw
Photography: Michelle Donner

INTRODUCTION

This book is designed especially for those who are just learning to read. The large type and simple language are intended to make this book engaging for young people, offering a bit of a challenge while at the same time, making it easy enough that early readers feel the joy of accomplishment with each page.

You'll notice at the bottom of every page a smaller and lighter text. This is included for older readers to help make this book a fun book to share—perhaps in a Buddy Reading program where older children read with younger ones, or maybe a parent or grandparent enjoying reading time with one of their favorite youngsters.

The bonus text at the bottom of every page will offer more detail to the "tour" and some interesting facts. Look for special 'WHEN YOU VISIT' highlights that will be useful for when you visit the site yourself.

The grounds at the Gamble Plantation Historic State Park are open seven days a week and it is free to walk around and see the homes and Visitor's Center. (The Visitor's Center and Mansion are closed on Tuesdays and Wednesdays, but guests can still walk the grounds.) Tours are very inexpensive and informative. Ticket sales help maintain this beautiful historic landmark.

ABIGAIL ROSE VISITS
The Gamble Plantation

AN EARLY READER ADVENTURE

Abigail Rose at the Mansion's Front Door

Hello!

My name is Abigail Rose.

Today I am touring an old home.

Will you come with me?

Abigail Rose is touring the Gamble Mansion at the Gamble Plantation Historic State Park in Ellenton, Florida. This is the oldest building on the peninsula (the part that points down) of the state of Florida. It was built between 1845-1850.

You and your family can go visit this historic site. Because it is a Florida State Park, there are friendly Park Rangers who offer tours and can answer questions. There is even a small museum in the Visitor's Center and a place to picnic behind the house.

This house is bigger than mine.

It has tall white columns all around it.

The house was built a long time ago.

It once belonged to a man named Major Robert Gamble.

That's why it is called the Gamble Mansion.

Major Robert Gamble moved to this area from Tallahassee, where his family members were prominent bankers and plantation owners. They originally came from Virginia. He and his brother decided to move here and try to grow sugarcane. Sugarcane grew well here and money was good... for a while.

Major Gamble loved this house. One of its architects was an architect for the White House in Washington, D.C. Can you find me on the porch by the TALL column in the small photo?

Gamble Mansion, Ellenton, Florida; near Bradenton, Fla.

PLANS

FIRST FLOOR

WORK ROOM CARPENTER SHOP, ETC.

KITCHEN

SEC. ON C-C.

PASSAGE

PANTRY

DINING ROOM

VERANDA

HALL

PARLOR

VERANDA

HALL

VERANDA

SEE SHEET NO. 3

DIAM 2'-3" ± SHEET 5

—NOTE—
WALLS BUILT OF COQUINA BRICK, 4½" × 9½"; SHELL-LIME MORTAR. SEE SHEET #7. COLUMNS BUILT OF PIE-SHAPED COQUINA BRICK. SEE SHEET #7.

CEILING OVER PASSAGE AT A-A

SECOND FLOOR

SLAVES SEWING ROOM

MAJOR ROBERT GAMBLE'S BEDROOM

PASSAGE

CLOTHES PRESS

CEILING OVER PASSAGE 9'-0"

SEC. ON B-B

VERANDA

GUEST

VERANDA

JUDAH BENJAMIN ROOM

HALL

VERANDA

SCALE OF DETAILS

SCALE OF PLANS

METRIC

MEASURED BY DONALD CORLEY.
DRAWN BY H.C. DOZIER.

U.S. DEPARTMENT OF THE INTERIOR
OFFICE OF NATIONAL PARKS, BUILDINGS, AND RESERVATIONS
BRANCH OF PLANS AND DESIGN

NAME OF STRUCTURE

GAMBLE MANSION
FLORIDA—MANATEE COUNTY—MANATEE

SURVEY NO. FLA-112
6-15-35

HISTORIC AMERICAN BUILDINGS SURVEY
SHEET 2 OF 10 SHEETS

INDEX NO. FLA 41-ELTO, 1

9

Fresh Sugarcane and Sugar

Major Gamble and his workers planted sugarcane nearby.

Sugarcane is made into sugar and cane syrup.

People have always loved sugar.

Do you like sweets?

Sugarcane is still a major agricultural staple today. In Major Gamble's time it was quite a commodity, meaning people used it sparingly because it was expensive.

WHEN YOU VISIT: Make sure you have the Rangers tell you how the sugarcane was grown, harvested, and processed. Ask them where the Gamble Sugar Mill was and how you can drive by and see what remains of it today.

The house was built by hand.

Many men made bricks from something called *tabby*, which is made of oyster shells.

In the Visitor's Center, I saw the bricks used for the tall columns.

Each brick was shaped like a slice of pie.

It is hard to imagine hand stacking layers of pie-shaped bricks to create these enormous columns, but that is exactly how they were made. Visit the museum in the Visitor's Center to see what these bricks looked like.

WHEN YOU VISIT: Count the columns. How many do you see? You should count eighteen in all!

Pie-Shaped Tabby Bricks

The Entry Hall

Let's go inside the mansion!

Through the front doors we enter a hall.

To the left is a stairwell.

We will go upstairs later.

I wonder what is up there?

For nearly fifty years this was the only way up and down in this house. You will see the family who lived here much later added a second set of stairs near the back of the house. They were probably tired of all the kids running through the house to get to the only stairwell!

Visitors to the mansion would always enter the house through the front door. People were much more formal than we are today.

Through the front hall, to the right, is a long hallway with tall windows.

The windows are big!

And look how thick the walls are.

Why do you think the walls are so thick?

The house was built before electricity and air conditioning, therefore the use of many windows and thick walls meant the house could be made more comfortable. The thick walls insulated the house from both the heat and the cold. And the tall windows, set opposite one another, meant a constant gulf breeze could keep the air inside fresher and a little bit cooler. The porch, which wraps around the house, also shaded these windows, helping to keep the inside cool and protected from rain.

WHEN YOU VISIT: Notice how tall the ceilings are in this home. The tall ceilings helped cool the home as well by trapping heat up high, because heat rises!

The Downstairs Hallway and Windows

The Parlor

This room is called a *parlor*.

Guests would come here to see Major Gamble and maybe visit or have tea.

There were no radios or TVs then, so people played musical instruments, sang, played card games, or just talked to one another.

Imagine that!

This is where guests were received and business callers probably waited to see Major Gamble. That's him in the painting over the piano.

WHEN YOU VISIT: In this room, be sure to notice the tea caddy. It's the wooden box there on the table. It has a LOCK on it. The Ranger or tour guide will explain why... but I'll give you a hint: Not everyone at the time was able to offer tea to his or her guests.

Back down the hallway is the next room.

This is the dining room.

All the meals were eaten here.

During parties, the furniture would be moved out for dancing!

Major Robert Gamble, although a bachelor, would entertain guests with fancy dinners and celebrate in this room. There weren't many people to socialize with around here at the time. But we know Robert's family visited when they could, and local plantation owners probably called now and again. The gentleman in the portrait is his father, John Grattan Gamble.

WHEN YOU VISIT: Did you notice the picture rail where the wall meets the ceiling? This type of wall-hanging method was used well into the 20th century when houses had hard plaster on the interior walls, making it impossible to use nails. Hooks and wires enabled the homeowner to display paintings from the picture rail.

The Dining Room

The Kitchen Hearth

Food was cooked in the kitchen over an open fire in this huge fireplace.

Bread was baked. Chickens Roasted.

Notice the black *soot* on the wall above the *hearth?*

Imagine how HOT this room would be!

The kitchens for houses of this time were often built a few steps away and separate from the house. This was because of the danger of fire spreading into the main house. A fire was going in the kitchen hearth nearly 24 hours a day, every day of the year.

Without refrigeration, food was consumed usually within a very short time, except for breads (like that on the mantle), salted meat, pickled vegetables, and jarred produce. No leftovers here!

This was a very important room.

Here workers, usually slaves, would mend items or make candles.

That funny shaped thing above my head is a *candle mold*. Soap and candles weren't bought at a store. They were made right here.

That big block on the table is soap!

Without local stores like we have today, people relied mainly on hand-made items. Other things, like fabric and furniture, were purchased on trips by boat to Pensacola or New Orleans and were mended here until they had to be replaced.

WHEN YOU VISIT: See the metal bathtub leaning in the corner? A bath would be taken in a metal tub like this one. Water was warmed in the fireplace and poured into the tub. No faucet in here! Where did they get their water? Turn the page to find out.

The Work Room

The Cistern

26

This is called a *cistern*.

It collects rainwater from the roof of the mansion for people to drink.

People could not drink water from the river.

It is said that tiny fish were kept in the cistern to eat any insects and *algae* that would grow.

Don't catch a fish in your bucket!

There was little fresh water available in the area, so a system like this was necessary for survival. The cistern was large enough to hold 40,000 gallons of water, enough to support 175 people.

The water would pass from one end of the sloped cistern to the other and be filtered through the dividing wall and kept clean by the small fish. Pretty genius, huh?

WHEN YOU VISIT: Make sure you take a peek down into the cistern.

Here is another set of stairs added many years after the home was built.

The Patten Family bought the mansion and land around it in 1873.

They lived in the home for 25 years.

They were smart to add a second set of stairs, weren't they?

Robert Gamble sold the property in 1858 and moved back to Tallahassee where he later married and settled down for the remainder of his life.

The Pattens, from Savannah, Georgia, lost everything after the Civil War (War Between the States) and decided to start anew here on Gamble's old plantation. Major Patten divided the plantation into smaller parcels and gave one to each of his children, which created a small town. He named the town after his oldest daughter, Ellen. That's how Ellenton got its name.

WHEN YOU VISIT: George Patten designated the land just behind the mansion (on the other side of the tree line and culvert) as a cemetery for local residents. He and his whole family are buried there.

The Back Stairs

The Patten House

From the cistern we can see another house.

Mary and George Patten's son, Dudley, built it in 1895 for his wife Melville and their children.

Melville, "Mellie" or Mother Patten as she was also known, lived in this house until her death in 1966.

The Patten House started out with only four rooms. The dining room and kitchen were added in 1909. The second floor and porches were finished in 1912. It is called a Victorian-style home and many people love the "Gingerbread Trim" on the porches.

Soon, when the Patten House is fully restored, visitors can once again tour this community treasure—where people in the area would congregate, especially on Sundays after church, for sing-a-longs and cookouts. A favorite event was a "Chicken Pilau" where townsfolk would bring chicken and rice and boil it in the yard in huge kettles, then eat together picnic-style while the children played and adults caught up on news and gossip.

At the front of the Gamble Mansion is a bedroom that at one time overlooked the Manatee River.

Guests would often stay in this room.

This room is famous because a man named Judah P. Benjamin once stayed here.

Have you seen a bathroom yet?

The story of Judah P. Benjamin and his exciting escape at the end of the Civil War (War Between the States) is a fascinating one. He was able to escape to England from Sarasota Bay, thanks to the help of the local community here in Manatee County.

WHEN YOU VISIT: The reason this room no longer has a view of the river is because the trees have all grown up and there are many homes built on the other side of the road in front of the mansion. But at one time, there was a clear view all the way to the river and far beyond.

The Benjamin Bedroom

Washbasin and Chamber Pot

Isn't this pottery pretty?

Ready for a shock?

THIS is the bathroom.

The bottom pot is called a *chamber pot* and was used as a toilet. The top bowl was the sink where people washed up with water (from the cistern) in the pitcher.

It is nearly impossible to imagine NOT having an indoor bathroom like we have today. But for centuries, people used a *chamber pot* and *washbasin* like these. Of course, there was an outdoor toilet called an *outhouse*. But at night, or if someone was ill, this indoor alternative was the only way to take care of that kind of business. Ready for another shock? It was often the job for the youngest child in the house to empty the chamber pots!

This gentleman in uniform is one of the Florida State Park Rangers, named Ted.

It is the rangers' job to take care of the buildings, the grass, and the fences—everything here!

Rangers also give tours and are always ready to answer questions.

Be sure to say hello to them!

The Gamble Mansion was purchased in 1925 by the Judah P. Benjamin Chapter of the United Daughters of the Confederacy and donated to the State of Florida, who has overseen its care and preservation ever since. Members of local and state historical societies and a group called The Gamble Plantation Preservation Alliance assist the Rangers with these tasks.

Ranger Ted

Archeological Finds from the Plantation

In the Visitor's Center, look for this display.

People who study the items left behind from others who lived a long time ago are called *Archeologists.*

These people study things they find buried in the ground.

At Gamble Plantation, they found broken bottles, plates, and tools.

I see a child's toy. Do you see it?

Archeologists studied the plantation in the 1970s by measuring and plotting, then digging holes where they had measured and marked. The Visitor's Center has a display of these items, but many more are still being studied at local universities. By studying what people leave behind, we are able to better understand how and where they lived, what tools they used, as well as how and what they ate.

Abigail Rose in a Front Porch Rocking Chair

The Gamble Mansion has stood on this spot for over 170 years.

There were no paved roads when it was built, no electric lights, not even a car or a bicycle.

A lot has changed since this home was built.

I am glad you visited with me today. I hope you will go see it all for yourself!

The End

The park is opened to the public 365 days a year from 8AM until sunset. The home is open for tours Thursday through Monday, six times a day between 9AM and 5PM. Make sure you stop into the Visitor's Center for the museum and to purchase tickets. The Visitor's Center is that building behind me in the photo.

For more information please visit: **floridastateparks.org/park/Gamble-Plantation**.

WORDS YOU MAY NOT KNOW:

Algae - A group of simple plant-like organisms that often grow on wet rock.

Archeologist - Someone who studies the material remains (such as fossil relics, artifacts, and monuments) of past human life and activities.

Candle Mold - A cylinder-shaped container into which liquid wax is poured to make candles.

Cistern - An underground reservoir or tank for holding water.

Chamber Pot - A bowl-shaped container with a handle and often a lid, used as a portable toilet.

Hearth - The floor of a fireplace.

Mansion - A large dwelling house, typically one that is larger than most.

Outhouse - A small building, often built over a deep hole in the ground that people use as a non-flushing toilet.

Parlor - The front room of a home, usually the most fancy, used to visit with guests or host gatherings.

Soot – A black powdery substance made by a fire, often found near a fireplace.

Sugarcane - A tall grass that grows in tropical regions and is used for sugar and cane syrup production.

Tabby - A type of concrete made by burning oyster shells to create lime (a sticky substance), then mixing it with water, sand, ash, and broken oyster shells.

Washbasin - A large bowl, usually with an accompanying pitcher of water, used as a sink for washing one's hands and face.

This photo shows Side One of the Gamble Mansion and Plantation historical marker near the Visitor's Center.

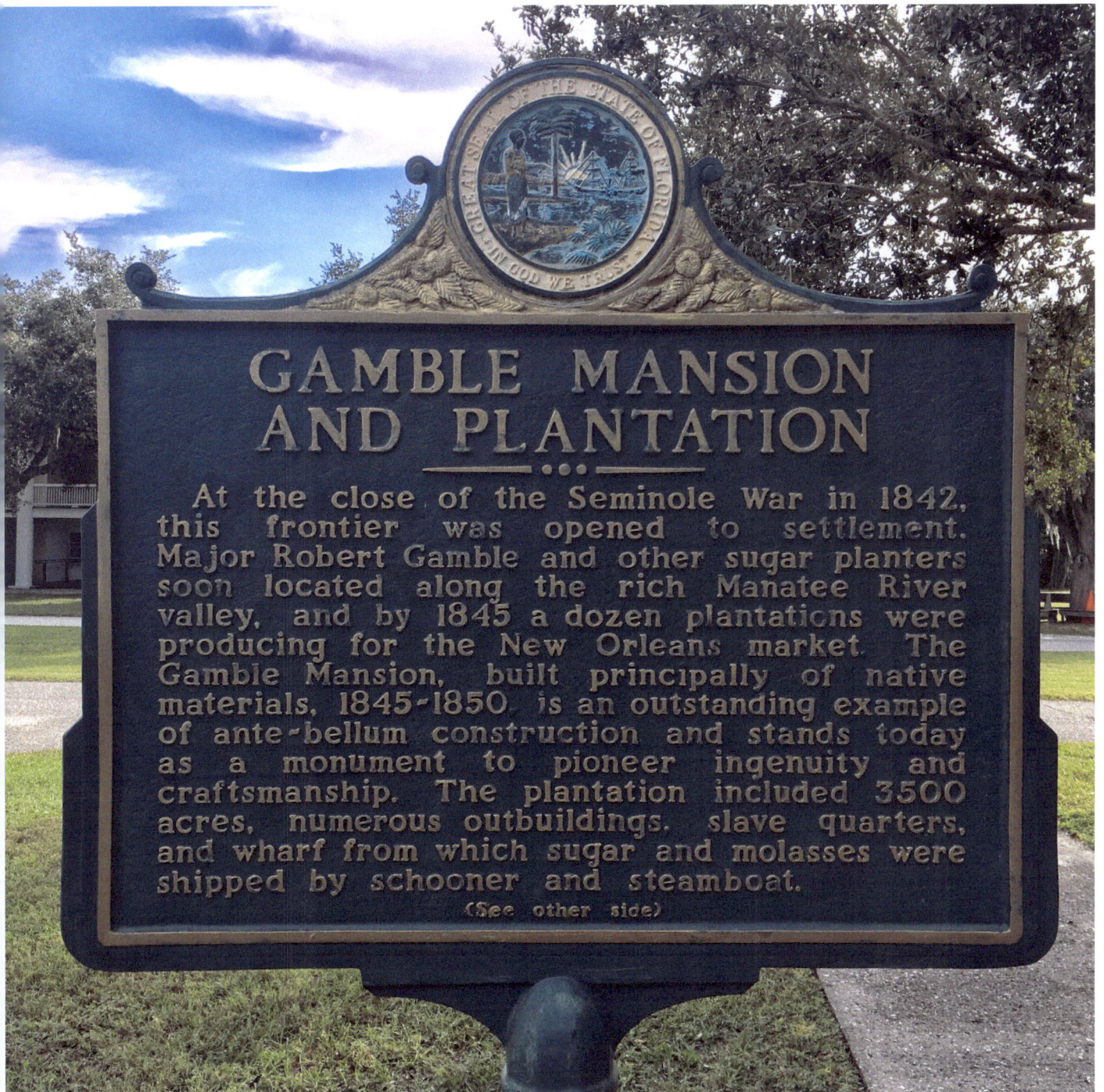

GAMBLE MANSION AND PLANTATION

At the close of the Seminole War in 1842, this frontier was opened to settlement. Major Robert Gamble and other sugar planters soon located along the rich Manatee River valley, and by 1845 a dozen plantations were producing for the New Orleans market. The Gamble Mansion, built principally of native materials, 1845-1850 is an outstanding example of ante-bellum construction and stands today as a monument to pioneer ingenuity and craftsmanship. The plantation included 3500 acres, numerous outbuildings, slave quarters, and wharf from which sugar and molasses were shipped by schooner and steamboat.

(See other side)

Historical Marker – Side One

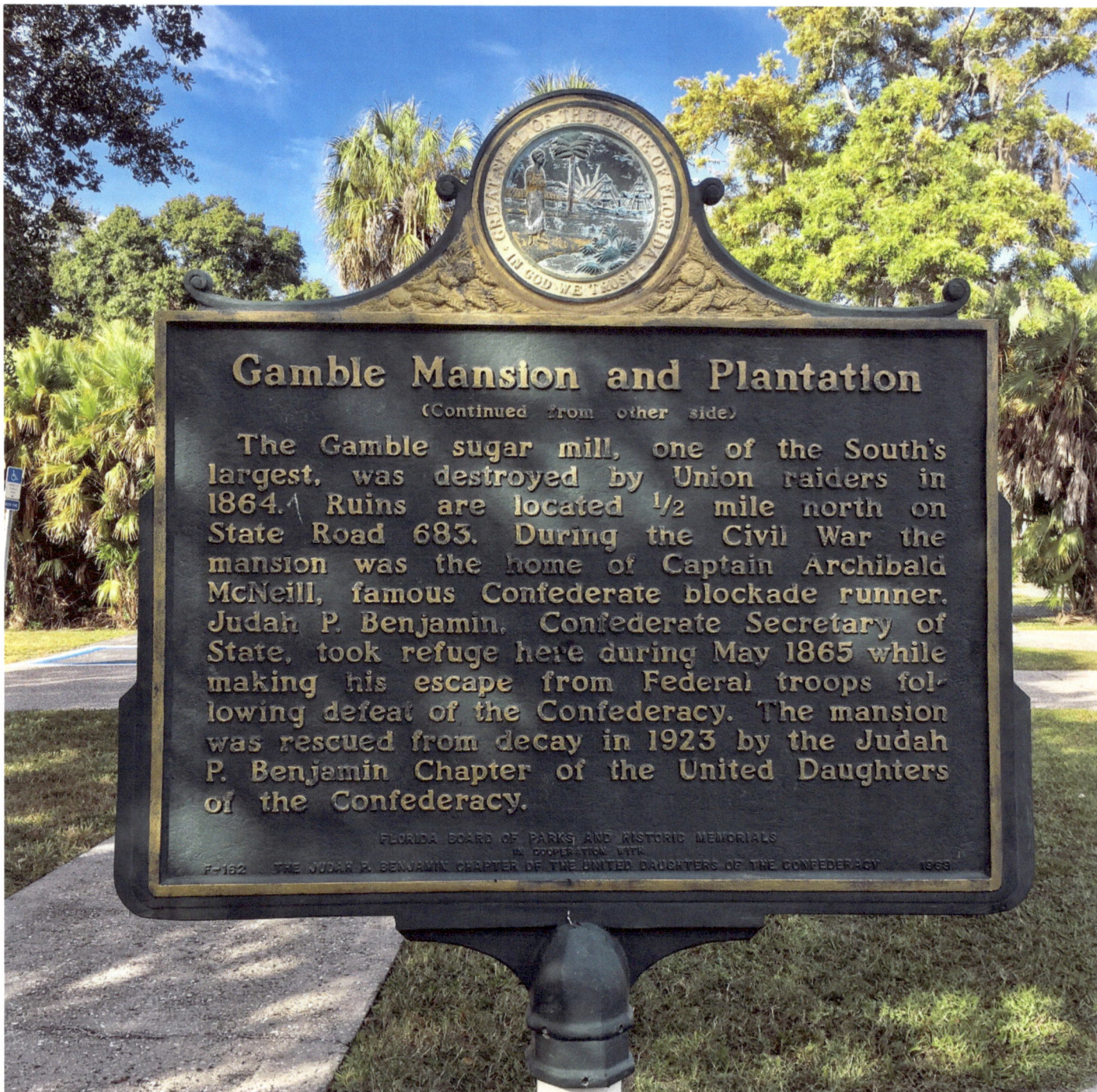

Gamble Mansion and Plantation
(Continued from other side)

The Gamble sugar mill, one of the South's largest, was destroyed by Union raiders in 1864. Ruins are located ½ mile north on State Road 683. During the Civil War the mansion was the home of Captain Archibald McNeill, famous Confederate blockade runner. Judah P. Benjamin, Confederate Secretary of State, took refuge here during May 1865 while making his escape from Federal troops following defeat of the Confederacy. The mansion was rescued from decay in 1923 by the Judah P. Benjamin Chapter of the United Daughters of the Confederacy.

FLORIDA BOARD OF PARKS AND HISTORIC MEMORIALS
IN COOPERATION WITH
F-162 THE JUDAH P. BENJAMIN CHAPTER OF THE UNITED DAUGHTERS OF THE CONFEDERACY 1969

Historical Marker – Side Two

IMPORTANT PEOPLE:

Major Robert Gamble (1813-1906) Son of Tallahassee banker, John Gamble, Robert moved to the Manatee Settlement in 1842 to start a sugar plantation. At one time it was the largest producer of sugarcane in the state. He sold the plantation in 1858 and lived the rest of his life in the Tallahassee area.

Judah P. Benjamin (1811-1884) Known as "the brains of the Confederacy" Benjamin served as Attorney General, Secretary of War, and Secretary of State for the Confederacy.

Mary (1819-1897) **& Major George Patten** (1806-1891) The Pattens had a plantation in Savannah, Georgia that was destroyed during 'Sherman's March to the Sea' near the end of the Civil War (War Between the States). The family moved to Florida and purchased the Gamble Plantation in 1873. (While they were waiting for the purchase to go through, the family lived in the old Braden Castle on the south side of the Manatee River, literally just south of the Gamble Plantation by boat.) Mary and George Patten lived in the Gamble Mansion for the remainder of their lives.

Melville (1868-1966) **& Dudley Patten** (1861-1919) Dudley was the youngest son of Mary and George Patten who purchased the Gamble Plantation in 1873. Dudley built the Patten House in 1895 for his family. What started out as a simple four-room cottage grew through additions to become the Victorian home we see today. His wife, "Mellie" or Mother Patten, lived there until she died in 1966, two years shy of her 100th birthday.

This photo shows Side Two of the Gamble Mansion and Plantation historical marker near the Visitor's Center.

SPECIAL THANKS:

Thank you to **Michelle Donner** for agreeing to be a part of this crazy idea for a book and for the magnificent photos. Thank you to my husband, **Mike Hartsaw,** and our children, **Emily & David,** who have all been super supportive of this project. Thanks always to my parents **Brenda and Tim Bell** and **Grant Rast,** for your love, support and "unbiased" praise. I especially appreciate the feedback from my friend, **Colleen Cosgrove**—having a Kindergarten teacher's perspective was phenomenal help. Many thanks to **Darrell King**—you have been a positive force in my life since the day I met you. Thank you to **Jan Greene,** president of the Judah P. Benjamin Chapter of the UDC, and to **Gail Jesse,** president of the Gamble Plantation Preservation Alliance, for your encouragement. Rangers **Kevin Kiser** and **Ted Unger,** to you I give a huge THANK YOU for your generous help and especially your patience.

Thank <u>you</u>, **Dear Reader,** for spending time inside this book. I hope it sparks your imagination as it gives you a glimpse of history. I hope you are inspired to learn more and to help preserve the past for generations to come.   — *Lela*

The photo at right is a Google Earth screenshot showing the **Gamble Plantation Historic State Park** and the area around it as it appears today. This is a great way to see the position of the mansion near the Manatee River. Remember, when Major Gamble and Major Patten each lived here, there was hardly anyone else here. There were no roads or highways. The best they had was probably a dirt path. There were no bridges then either, so people crossed the river by boat. What do you think these people would think if they saw the area today?

NOTE: On the map, in the bottom left corner, do you see the **Manatee Village Historical Park**? You should pay them a visit as well and learn what was going on at the same time in history on the south side of the river. Visit their webpage: *manateeclerk.com*

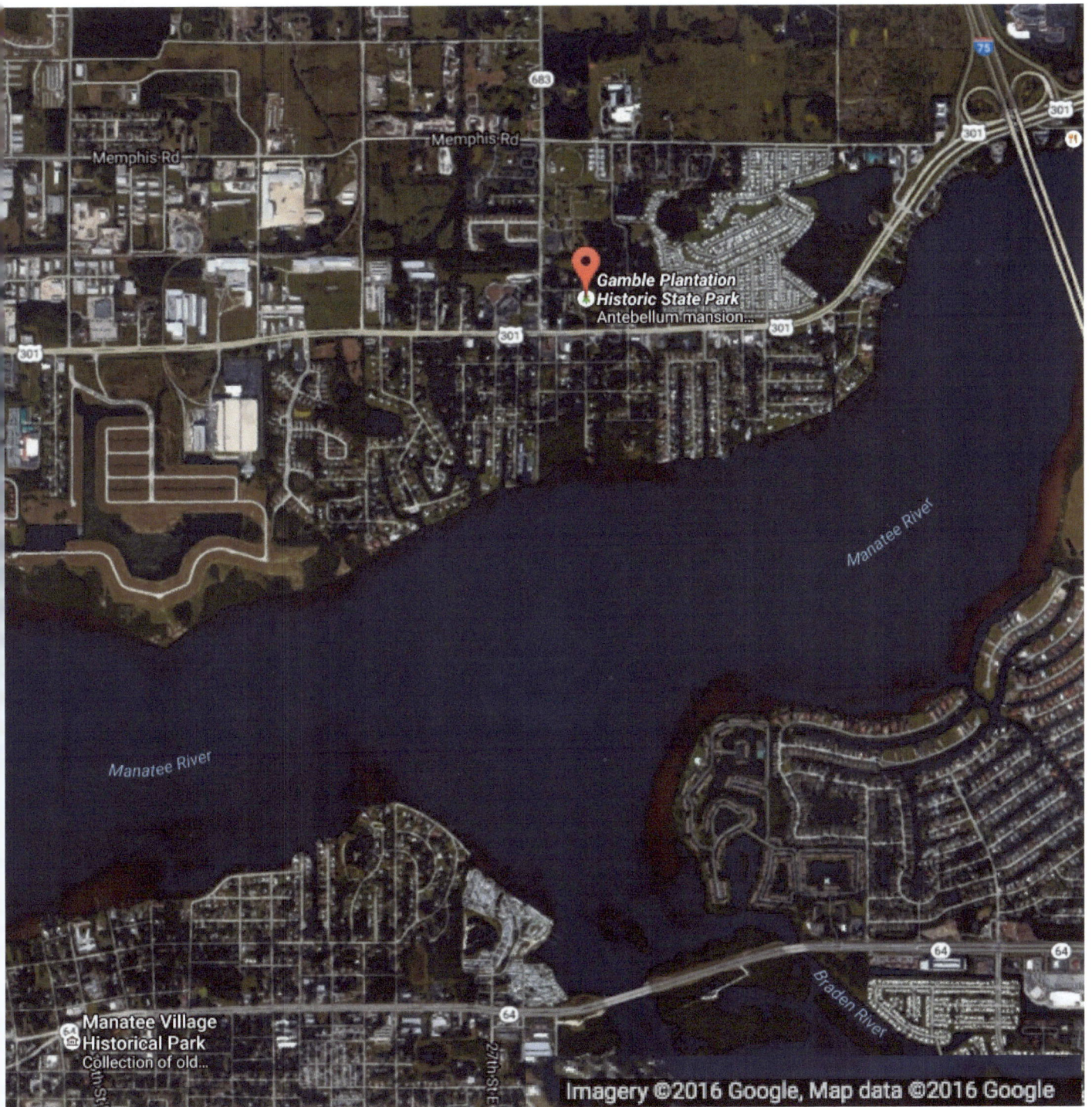

Aerial View of the Area Near the Gamble Plantation Historic State Park

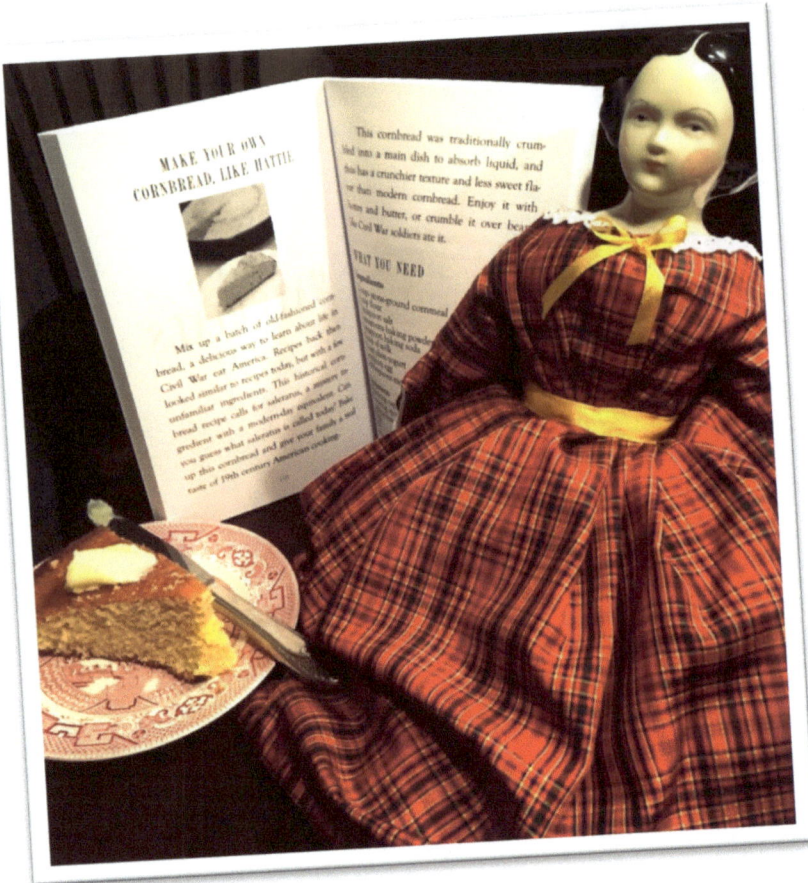

Look inside my first book, **The Adventures of Abigail Rose-Ida Patten's Antebellum Doll,** for a delightful work of historical fiction and plenty of fun historical facts PLUS bonus material like this recipe for corn bread from the 1800s that you can make yourself!

In the book, I tell the story of life on a 19th century sugar plantation, where I became lost! I saw and heard everything that went on there for almost fifty years!

You can find copies of the book at the following locations:

- The Gamble Plantation Historic State Park
- The South Florida Museum
- The Manatee Village Historical Park
- The Manatee County Agriculture Museum
- Retro Rosie's and Cobweb's Unique Finds
- The Maker's Market & Workshops
- DeSoto National Memorial Park
- Carnton & The Carter House, in Franklin, Tennessee

The book is also available on **Amazon.com**.

See you again, soon, I hope!
Love,
Abigail Rose

www.ingramcontent.com/pod-product-compliance
Lightning Source LLC
Chambersburg PA
CBHW041546040426
42447CB00002B/58